A Guide for Writing and Publishing Your Book in 90-Days

GERMAINE MILLER-SUMMERS

90-DAY BOOK CREATION™
A Guide for Writing and Publishing Your Book in 90-Days

HOV Publishing is a division of HOV, LLC.
email: hopeofvision@gmail.com
www.hovpub.com
www.90daybookcreation.com
email: 90daybookcreation@gmail.com

Front Cover Design and Inside layout by HOV Design Solutions
Editing: HOVP Editing Team and AI Research

ISBN Paperback: 978-1-955107-54-9
ISBN Hard Case: 978-1-955107-55-6
ISBN eBook: 978-1-955107-53-2

Printed in the United States of America

This book, structured over twelve chapters, can be used as a roadmap for aspiring authors who are looking to write and publish their work in a 90-day timeframe. By following this guide, authors can navigate the complexities of the publishing world and bring their ideas to life.

Writing and publishing a book in 90 days is an aggressive timeline. While it's definitely feasible to get the bulk of writing and preliminary editing done, some aspects (like professional editing, layout, and printing) may take longer. Adjustments might need to be made based on individual situations.

Start your journey with a single word and arrive at your destination with a book. ~ Germaine Miller-Summers

CONTENTS

7. Personal Branding
8. Public Appearances and Events
9. Licensing and Foreign Rights
10. Regularly Update and Market

1. AI for Research and Information Gathering
2. Writing Aids and Grammar Checkers
3. Plot Development and World Building
4. Productivity Boosters
5. AI as Co-Writer
6. Design and Layout
7. Audience Targeting and Marketing

- Reflecting on the 90-day journey
- The lifelong journey of an author
- Encouraging continued growth and exploration
- The empowerment of becoming an author

- Checklists and timelines
- Sample outlines and writing schedules
- Sample 90-day writing and publishing calendar
- Templates: Email pitches, press releases, etc.
- Different Types of Advertising
- Advertising Resources and Tools

INTRODUCTION

In a world saturated with tasks, ideas, and ambitions, our greatest challenge often isn't generating inspiration but bringing these dreams to life. As our digital age has given rise to a culture of instant gratification, the fundamental principles of dedication, time management, and swift execution have become paramount. This book seeks to explore and decode these principles by exploring four pivotal areas.

First, we'll shed light on the importance of setting a deadline. A deadline, often seen as a pressure point, is in reality a beacon that guides our efforts and organizes our priorities. It serves as a tangible reminder of our commitment and drives us to action when procrastination waits in the shadows. A deadline isn't just a date on a calendar; it's a promise to ourselves.

From there, we'll zoom into the effectiveness of the 90-day timeframe. Not too short to be superficial, yet not too long to become overwhelming, 90 days strike a balance that facilitates focused effort and real progress. This golden window offers both the urgency and the flexibility required to birth meaningful projects.

Our discovery will then move to the realm of publishing quickly. In an era of information overload, timing can be everything. We'll analyze why speed, when complemented by quality, can be a game-changer in the dissemination of ideas, capturing audiences, and establishing credibility.

Finally, we'll confront the myths and realities surrounding the feasibility of a 90-day journey. Many have reservations: Is it too ambitious? Is quality compromised? By comparing the misconceptions with real-world examples and tangible results, we aim to reveal the process and offer a clear, actionable roadmap.

As we navigate through these focal points, readers will not only be equipped with the tools and insights to harness the power of deadlines, but they will also be empowered to make the most of every opportunity, dispelling myths and realizing the full potential of what can be achieved in a focused 90-day period. Welcome to a journey that promises transformation, acceleration, and a reimagining of what's feasible.

CHAPTER
ONE
PREPARATION and MINDSET

In the journey of authorship, your first step is not putting pen to paper or fingers to keys. It's setting a firm foundation and the right frame of mind. When you begin with preparation and the proper mindset, you pave the way for success, enabling you to tackle challenges with resilience and navigate the world of writing with finesse. Let's dive deep into the essentials of this groundwork.

1. Defining Your 'Why'

Every masterpiece has a reason behind its creation. Before embarking on your writing journey, ask yourself: *Why am I doing this?* Your 'why' is the core motivation driving you to write. It's the flame that keeps you going through the darkest of writer's blocks. Whether it's to inspire, educate, entertain, or simply to express, understanding your 'why' gives purpose to your words.

_____

_____

_____

_____

_____

Exercise: Write down three reasons why you want to write this book. Reflect on them whenever you need motivation.

_____

_____

_____

_____

_____

_____

_____

2. Picking Your Topic

Choosing the right topic is crucial. It should resonate with your 'why' and ignite your passion. Ask yourself:

- What do I love talking about?

_____

_____

- What subject can I shed light on?

_____

_____

_____

- Is there a gap in the market for this topic?

_____

_____

Your topic should be a blend of your passion, expertise, and market demand.

3. Setting Measurable Goals

"Write a book" is a noble aim, but it's vague. Break it down:

- How many words or chapters do I plan to write daily or weekly?

- By when do I want to finish my first draft?

- How much time can I dedicate to writing daily?

Setting specific, measurable, attainable, relevant, and time-bound (SMART) goals will give you a clear roadmap.

List your goals:

_____

_____

_____

_____

_____

4. The Foundation of a Successful Author

Becoming a successful author is not just about writing skills. It's a mindset:

- **Resilience:** Embrace rejections and critiques. They're stepping stones, not setbacks.

- **Consistency:** Writing is a marathon, not a sprint. Regularity trumps intensity.

- **Curiosity:** Always be willing to learn. Dive deep into research, attend workshops, or join writing groups.

5. Setting Clear Goals and Intentions

While measurable goals provide a roadmap, clear intentions set the tone for your journey. Ask yourself:

- What emotions do I want to evoke in my readers?

  _____

  _____

- How do I want to grow as a writer during this process?

  _____

  _____

  _____

Let these intentions guide your narrative and voice.

_____

_____

_____

_____

_____

_____

_____

6. Cultivating Daily Writing Habits

A masterpiece is built one word at a time. Cultivate a daily writing habit:

- **Sacred Space:** Dedicate a spot for writing. Over time, just sitting there will prime your mind to write.

- **Set a Routine:** Whether it's 500 words, a page, or an hour – commit to it daily.

- **Minimize Distractions:** Put your phone on airplane mode or use apps that block distractions.

7. Tools and Resources for Efficient Writing

Thankfully, in our digital age, there are numerous tools to aid in your writing journey:

- **Word Processors:** Software like Microsoft Word or Google Docs are basic. For more advanced features, Scrivener is a popular choice.

  Scrivener is the go-to app for writers of all kinds, used every day by best-selling novelists, screenwriters, non-fiction writers, students, academics, ...

  What is the difference between Scrivener and word? Scrivener is designed for writers. The entire app has been created to make composing long-form documents efficient and practical. In Word, you create long documents, or a lot of smaller documents, such as one per chapter.

- **Distraction-Free Writing Apps:** Apps like 'FocusWriter' or 'OmmWriter' offer a clean writing environment.

  FocusWriter is a simple, distraction-free writing environment. It utilizes a hide-away interface that you access by moving your mouse to the edges of the screen, allowing the program to have a familiar look and feel to it while still getting out of the way so that you can immerse yourself in your work.

OmmWriter is a tool that makes writing a pleasure again, allowing users to be alone with their thoughts; to concentrate and to write without distractions. More than a word processor, OmmWriter is a place to get inspired.

- **Research and Note-Taking:** Evernote or OneNote are great for organizing your thoughts and research.

- **Writing Communities:** Join online forums for writers like Absolute Write or Writer's Digest Community for feedback and camaraderie.

  Writer's Digest is an American magazine aimed at beginning and established writers. It contains interviews, market listings, calls for manuscripts, and how-to articles.

Conclusion:

In conclusion, preparation is more than just a step; it's your foundation. With the right mindset, you not only start your writing journey but also ensure you see it through to its destination. In the next chapter, we'll delve into the art and craft of writing, but always remember: the mindset you cultivate now will determine your journey's ease and success.

Notes:

_____

_____

_____

_____

_____

_____

_____

_____

_____

_____

_____

_____

_____

_____

_____

_____

_____

_____

_____

_____

_____

Notes:

Notes:

_____

_____

_____

_____

_____

_____

_____

_____

_____

_____

_____

_____

_____

_____

_____

_____

_____

_____

Notes:

_____

_____

_____

_____

_____

_____

_____

_____

_____

_____

_____

_____

_____

_____

_____

_____

_____

_____

_____

_____

CHAPTER
TWO

PLANNING your BOOK

1. Mind Mapping Your Ideas

Mind mapping is a free-form method of brainstorming that can help you visualize the entirety of your book and its many potential branches. Think of your book idea as the central node, and from there, let your thoughts branch out in all directions.

Tools: You can use pen and paper, a whiteboard, or digital tools like MindMeister or XMind.

MindMeister's easy-to-use, web-based mind map maker provides an infinite canvas for brainstorming, note taking, project planning and countless other creative ... https://www.mindmeister.com/

XMind is an idea management and mind mapping solution that helps businesses streamline operations related to brainstorming, data filtering, organization charting and more on a centralized platform. https://xmind.app/

How to Start: (create a list first before drawing it out)

- Place your main idea in the center.

  _____

  _____

- Branch out major themes or sub-topics from that main idea.

  _____

- From those themes, branch out supporting ideas or sections.

---

2. Structuring Your Book: From Mind Map to Chapter Breakdown

Once your mind map is complete, it's time to take a step back and discern a natural order or flow.

Chapter Creation:

- Look at your main branches. These are potential chapters or major sections of your book.

- The sub-branches become sub-chapters or key points within those chapters.

_____

_____

_____

_____

3. Setting a Daily Word Count Goal

Having a daily goal keeps you accountable and gives a tangible metric to work towards.

Determining Your Goal:

- Consider your timeline: When would you like the first draft done?

_____

_____

_____

- Consider your stamina: How much can you realistically write each day?

_____

_____

_____

- Adjust as needed: Your goal isn't set in stone. Adjust based on what you discover about your writing process.

_____

_____

_____

4. Identifying Your Book's Niche

It's essential to understand who you're writing for and what makes your book unique.

How to Identify:

- Research existing books in your general topic.

  _____

  _____

  _____

- Pinpoint what makes your approach or perspective different.

  _____

  _____

- Consider who would benefit most from your unique take.

  _____

  _____

5. Creating a Robust Book Outline

Your book's outline is like a road map, guiding you from start to finish.

Steps:

- Use your mind map as a starting point (refer to #2).

- Flesh out each chapter with key points, using the sub-branches from your mind map (refer to #2).

- Include introductory and concluding thoughts for each chapter.

_____

_____

_____

_____

_____

_____

_____

_____

_____

_____

_____

6. Setting Milestones: Breaking Your Book into Manageable Sections

By setting milestones, you can celebrate small achievements and prevent feeling overwhelmed.

Tips:

- Consider breaking it down by sections: introduction, early chapters, mid-point, climax, and conclusion.

_____

_____

_____

_____

_____

_____

- Reward yourself when you reach each milestone. It's a marathon, not a sprint.

_____

_____

_____

_____

_____

_____

7. Time Management Tips and Techniques

A book doesn't write itself. Here are tips to help you stay on track:

- **Set a Specific Time**: Decide on a dedicated writing time every day.

_____

_____

- **Remove Distractions**: Find a quiet place, or use apps like Focus@Will to enhance concentration.

   focus@will is a neuroscience based tool that uses specially sequenced instrumental music to increase your focus up to 400% when working and studying. Our tool helps extend your productivity cycle and effortlessly zones out distraction. Join 1,500,000 users today. It works! Get a free focus trial today! www.focusatwill.com

https://www.youtube.com/c/Focusatwill

- **Prioritize Tasks**: Before starting, know what sections or chapters you're targeting.

_____

_____

_____

_____

_____

- **Breaks are Essential**: Use the Pomodoro technique or similar methods to ensure you're giving yourself time to rest and rejuvenate.

THE POMODORO TECHNIQUE

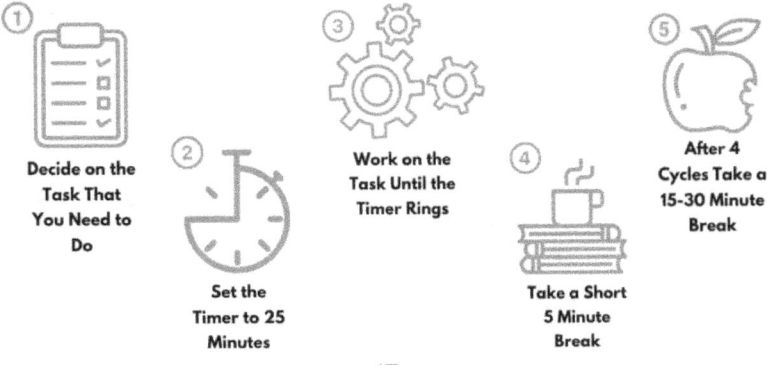

1. Decide on the Task That You Need to Do
2. Set the Timer to 25 Minutes
3. Work on the Task Until the Timer Rings
4. Take a Short 5 Minute Break
5. After 4 Cycles Take a 15-30 Minute Break

17

Conclusion:

In conclusion, the planning phase is just as critical, if not more so, than the actual writing. It sets the foundation and direction for your book, ensuring a coherent and organized flow of ideas. With proper planning, the writing process becomes a lot smoother and more enjoyable.

Notes:

_____

_____

_____

_____

_____

_____

_____

_____

_____

_____

_____

_____

_____

Notes:

_____

_____

_____

_____

_____

_____

_____

_____

_____

_____

_____

_____

_____

_____

_____

_____

_____

_____

_____

_____

_____

Notes:

Notes:

_____

_____

_____

_____

_____

_____

_____

_____

_____

_____

_____

_____

_____

_____

_____

_____

_____

_____

_____

Notes:

_____

_____

_____

_____

_____

_____

_____

_____

_____

_____

_____

_____

_____

_____

_____

_____

_____

_____

_____

CHAPTER
THREE

DIVE into WRITING

1. Setting up a dedicated writing space.

When it comes to diving into the world of writing, the environment plays a significant role. It's not just about having a desk and a computer; it's about creating a space that inspires and nurtures your creativity.

Tips for setting up your space:

- **Choose the Right Spot:** It doesn't have to be a separate room but a quiet corner can work wonders. If you're someone who gets inspired by nature, maybe a spot near the window would work best.

  _____

  _____

- **Eliminate Distractions:** This might mean putting your phone on airplane mode or using apps that block distracting websites (refer to Chapter 2 #7).

- **Personalize:** Add objects that inspire you, like books, paintings, or even a plant. These items can provide subconscious motivation and make your workspace feel like your own.

  _____

  _____

2. The importance of routine.

Routine provides structure, and for writers, this can translate into productivity. A set routine conditions the mind to get into the "writing zone" faster. Whether it's writing first thing in the morning or late at night, stick to a schedule that suits you.

3. Techniques for overcoming writer's block.

Every writer, at some point, faces the dreaded writer's block. It's that frustrating time when, no matter how hard you try, the words just won't flow. But fret not, there are ways to push past this.

- **Take a Break:** Sometimes the best thing you can do is step away for a bit.

- **Free Write:** Write about anything and everything that comes to your mind.

- **Mind Maps:** Visualize your ideas; this can help in connecting the dots.

- **Change Your Environment:** A change of scenery can reignite inspiration.

- **Read:** Reading can provide a fresh perspective and kickstart your writing juices

4. Writing the first draft: Quantity over quality.

The first draft is not about perfection. It's about getting your thoughts down on paper. Don't overthink; just write. It's easier to work with a bad page than a blank one. You can always edit a rough draft, but you can't edit what you haven't written.

5. Establishing a daily word count target.

Having a word count goal can be an effective way to maintain consistent progress. It can be as little as 500 words or as many as 5,000. The key is to find a number that is challenging yet achievable, and stick to it.

6. Staying motivated and accountable.

It's not always easy to stay motivated, especially when writing can sometimes feel isolating. Joining a writers' group, finding a writing buddy, or even sharing your progress on social media can help in holding you accountable.

7. Ensuring consistency in tone and style.

Your writing tone and style define your unique voice. To ensure consistency:

- **Create a Style Guide:** List down the nuances of your writing. This can be about punctuation, the spellings you prefer, or the tone you want to adopt.

  What are the key elements of a style guide?

  It covers aspects such as grammar, spelling, punctuation, terminology, voice, tone, structure, layout, and design. A content style guide helps you ensure that your content is clear, accurate, and consistent across all channels and platforms.

  What are the three major style guides?

  The most frequently used style guides in academic writing include the Publication Manual of the American Psychological Association (APA), the Modern Language Association's MLA Style Manual, and the Chicago Manual of Style (CMOS).

You are likely to encounter at least one of these styles when doing academic research.

_____

_____

_____

_____

- **Read Aloud:** Hearing your work can help you identify inconsistencies.

- **Seek Feedback:** Sometimes, an external perspective can catch what you might have missed.

Conclusion:

As you dive deeper into your writing journey, always remember why you started. The world needs your stories, your insights, and your unique voice. Embrace the challenges as they come and celebrate every small victory. Happy writing!

Notes:

_____

_____

_____

_____

_____

_____

Notes:

_____

_____

_____

_____

_____

_____

_____

_____

_____

_____

_____

_____

_____

_____

_____

_____

_____

_____

_____

Notes:

_____

_____

_____

_____

_____

_____

_____

_____

_____

_____

_____

_____

_____

_____

_____

_____

_____

_____

_____

Notes:

Notes:

_____

_____

_____

_____

_____

_____

_____

_____

_____

_____

_____

_____

_____

_____

_____

_____

_____

_____

CHAPTER
FOUR

EDITING and POLISHING

1. The Importance of Self-Editing

Before your manuscript goes out into the world, it deserves careful scrutiny. Self-editing is the process of revising and correcting your own work. It is not only about fixing errors, but also refining the prose and ensuring consistency. Here are a few reasons why this step is so crucial:

- **Clarity and Coherence**: Self-editing ensures your ideas are conveyed clearly and logically, making the narrative engaging for the reader.

- **Credibility**: Mistakes can undermine your credibility. By meticulously editing your work, you present yourself as a diligent and trustworthy author.

- **Efficiency**: Self-editing reduces the time and money spent on professional editing later on, as it ensures you're handing over a cleaner manuscript.

2. Techniques for Effective Self-Editing

- **Take a Break**: After finishing your draft, take a break. Returning to your work with fresh eyes will help you spot errors and inconsistencies more easily.

- **Read Aloud**: This technique allows you to catch awkward phrasings and inconsistencies.

- **Reverse Reading**: Start from the last sentence and work your way to the beginning. This helps in catching errors since it disrupts the narrative flow, making you focus on each sentence individually.

- **Use Technology**: Software like Grammarly, Hemingway, or ProWritingAid can help identify basic errors, passive voice, or overused words.

- **Print a Hard Copy**: Sometimes, errors become more apparent when reading from a physical paper.

3. **When and How to Hire a Professional Editor**

When you've done all you can on your own and want an expert's eyes, it's time to hire a professional. Here's how:

- **Decide What Type of Editor You Need**: There are developmental editors, copy editors, and proofreaders, each with a specific focus. Determine which is best for your needs.

- **Check Credentials and Ask for Samples**: Before hiring, ask for credentials, reviews, or sample edits.

- **Establish a Clear Agreement**: This should include the scope of work, timeline, and payment details.

- **Be Open to Feedback**: A professional editor's critique will be invaluable. Be receptive to changes and suggestions.

4. **Peer Review and Gathering Feedback**

Feedback from peers or beta readers can offer valuable perspectives.

- **Select a Diverse Group**: Choose readers from different backgrounds and reading preferences to get a wide range of feedback.

- **Provide Specific Questions**: Instead of a general "What did you think?", ask specific questions about plot development, character consistency, pacing, etc.

- **Review Feedback Collectively**: Sometimes feedback can be conflicting. Look for patterns in the comments to decide which changes to make.

5. **Formatting Your Book**

Presentation matters. Proper formatting ensures your book looks professional and is easy to read.

- **Consider the Platform**: If you're self-publishing, platforms like Amazon's Kindle (KDP) have specific formatting guidelines.

- **Font and Size**: Stick to easy-to-read fonts like Times New Roman or Arial. For print, a 12-point size is standard.

- **Consistent Headers and Footers**: Ensure chapter titles and page numbers are consistent in style and placement.

- **Spacing and Margins**: Typically, a 1-inch margin all around and a line spacing of 1.5 is preferred.

- **Professional Software**: Tools like Adobe InDesign or Scrivener can help with more sophisticated formatting needs.

Conclusion:

In conclusion, the journey from writing to publishing is a meticulous process. By dedicating time to editing and polishing, you ensure your book resonates with its intended audience and stands out in the literary world.

Notes:

_____

_____

_____

_____

_____

_____

_____

_____

_____

_____

_____

_____

_____

_____

Notes:

Notes:

_____

_____

_____

_____

_____

_____

_____

_____

_____

_____

_____

_____

_____

_____

_____

_____

_____

_____

_____

_____

CHAPTER
FIVE

COVER DESIGN and LAYOUT

1. Importance of a Professional Cover

A book cover is often the first point of contact for potential readers. Think of it as the packaging for your story. Just as consumers judge products by their packaging, readers judge a book by its cover.

- **First Impressions Matter**: A professionally designed cover creates a positive initial impression. It tells readers that the content inside has been given just as much care and attention.

- **Relevance to the Genre**: A cover that adheres to the conventions of its genre can indicate to readers that the book provides the kind of content they're looking for.

- **Standing Out in a Crowd**: In today's saturated book market, having a unique and professional cover can make your book stand out among thousands.

2. DIY Cover Design vs. Hiring a Designer

- **DIY (Do It Yourself)**:
    - **Pros**: Cost-effective, full control over the design, and a sense of personal accomplishment.
    - **Cons**: May not look professional, time-consuming, and can be a steep learning curve.

- **Hiring a Designer**:

  - **Pros**: Professional outcome, saves time, and the designer brings experience and an external perspective.

  - **Cons**: Can be costly and requires effective communication to ensure your vision is realized.

3. **Key Elements of an Attractive Book Cover**

- **Title**: Make sure it's legible and stands out. Your title should be easily read even in thumbnail size.

- **Imagery**: The image or graphic should resonate with the content of the book and the intended audience. Avoid cliches.

- **Typography**: Choose fonts that are readable and fit the mood of your book.

- **Colors**: Colors evoke emotions. Choose a palette that fits the tone of your story.

- **Back Cover**: This should include a blurb, author bio, and ISBN. The blurb should be engaging and make readers want to dive in.

4. **Typesetting and Interior Layout**

Beyond the cover, the interior layout is crucial for ensuring a pleasant reading experience.

- **Margins**: Ensure there's adequate space around the text to prevent the content from looking cramped.

- **Font and Size**: Choose a legible font. Classics like Times New Roman or Garamond are safe bets for most texts.

- **Line Spacing**: Ensure there's adequate spacing between lines for readability.

- **Headers and Footers**: Include page numbers, book titles, or chapter titles for easy navigation.

- **Chapter Start**: Starting chapters on a new page, possibly with a distinctive design or font, adds to the reader's experience.

5. **Using Tools Like Canva, Adobe InDesign, etc.**

- **Canva**: This is a user-friendly tool great for beginners. It offers customizable templates and is excellent for simple designs. The free version provides a vast array of options, while the pro version offers even more flexibility and resources.

- **Adobe InDesign**: This is a professional tool used by many designers for both cover design and interior layout. It offers a higher level of customization and is perfect for creating a truly professional look.

- **Other Tools**: Tools like GIMP (a free Photoshop alternative) or Scribus (a free InDesign alternative) can also be considered, depending on your proficiency and budget.

Conclusion:

In conclusion, a book's design, both cover, and layout are crucial elements that contribute to its success. Investing time, effort, and sometimes money into these aspects can significantly enhance a reader's experience and the book's overall reception in the market.

Notes:

_____

_____

_____

_____

_____

_____

_____

_____

_____

_____

_____

_____

_____

Notes:

_____

_____

_____

_____

_____

_____

_____

_____

_____

_____

_____

_____

_____

_____

_____

_____

_____

_____

_____

_____

Notes:

_____

_____

_____

_____

_____

_____

_____

_____

_____

_____

_____

_____

_____

_____

_____

_____

_____

_____

_____

Notes:

_____

_____

_____

_____

_____

_____

_____

_____

_____

_____

_____

_____

_____

_____

_____

_____

_____

_____

_____

_____

Notes:

_____

_____

_____

_____

_____

_____

_____

_____

_____

_____

_____

_____

_____

_____

_____

_____

_____

_____

CHAPTER
SIX

FORMATTING and PLATFORMS

1. **E-book Formatting 101**

Introduction to E-book Formats:

E-books come in various formats, with the most popular ones being EPUB (Electronic Publication) and MOBI. EPUB is accepted by almost every e-reading platform and device except Amazon Kindle, which uses MOBI.

Basic Principles:

- **Consistent Typography:** Ensure the same font type and size for all similar elements, such as headings and body text.

- **Use Styles:** Rather than manually bolding or italicizing text, use style settings to ensure consistency.

- **Spacing:** Avoid multiple consecutive line breaks; use spacing settings instead.

- **Links:** Test hyperlinks to ensure they direct the reader to the right place.

2. **Print Book Formatting Basics**

Determining Book Size:
This is usually the first step. Sizes might include 5"x8", 6"x9", or larger for textbooks and manuals.

Key Considerations:

- **Margins:** Allow for adequate margins, especially in the gutter (where the book binds).

- **Pagination:** Odd-numbered pages are always on the right.

- **Headers and Footers:** These can include the book title, chapter title, and page numbers.

- **Images:** High-resolution images are a must. Consider bleed if the image runs off the edge of the page.

3. Considering Audiobook Versions

Narration:
Your choice of narrator can influence how listeners perceive your story. Consider professional narrators or voice actors.

Technical Aspects:

- **Quality:** Record in a soundproof room to eliminate background noise.

- **Editing:** Edit out long pauses, mistakes, and other extraneous sounds.

- **Consistency:** Ensure that the volume and pace remain consistent throughout the book.

Benefits of Audiobooks:

In our busy world, many prefer listening over reading. Offering your work as an audiobook can tap into this large audience.

4. Tools and Resources for Seamless Formatting

- **Calibre:** A free, open-source tool for e-book library management, which allows for e-book format conversion.

- **Scrivener:** A popular writing software that offers features for manuscript formatting and exports directly to EPUB or MOBI.

- **Vellum:** A software for Mac users, making it easy to create beautifully formatted e-books and print books.

- **InDesign:** Adobe's professional page design and layout toolset, commonly used for print book formatting.

- **ACX (Audiobook Creation Exchange):** Owned by Amazon, it's a marketplace for authors, narrators, and producers. You can find professionals here to help with audiobook production.

Tips for Choosing the Right Tool:

- **Budget:** Some tools are free, while others require a significant investment.

- **Skill Level:** If you're new, choose user-friendly software with good community support.

- **End Goal:** Consider where you're publishing. Some platforms have specific requirements.

Conclusion:

In conclusion, no matter which format you choose for your book, ensure that it provides the best possible reading or listening experience for your audience. Investing time and possibly money in formatting can make the difference between a good book and a great one.

Notes:

_____

_____

_____

_____

_____

_____

_____

_____

_____

_____

_____

_____

_____

_____

_____

Notes:

_____

_____

_____

_____

_____

_____

_____

_____

_____

_____

_____

_____

_____

_____

_____

_____

_____

_____

_____

_____

Notes:

CHAPTER
SEVEN

ISBN, COPYRIGHT, and LEGALITIES

1. The Purpose and Process of Obtaining an ISBN

Purpose of an ISBN:
The International Standard Book Number (ISBN) is a unique identifier for books. An ISBN helps retailers, libraries, distributors, and readers find your book, ensuring that they are purchasing or borrowing the correct edition or format.

Process of Obtaining an ISBN:

- Determine how many ISBNs you need. Remember that each format of your book (e.g., hardcover, paperback, ebook) requires a separate ISBN.

- In the U.S., you can purchase ISBNs from Bowker at myidentifiers.com. In other countries, you might need to approach the designated ISBN agency.

- Register your book details and ensure all information is accurate.

2. Understanding and Registering for Copyright

Understanding Copyright:
Copyright is a legal right that grants the creator of an original work exclusive rights to its distribution, reproduction, and adaptation.

Registering for Copyright:

While copyright is automatic upon the creation of a work, registering provides legal advantages. In the U.S.:

- Visit the U.S. Copyright Office website. https://www.copyright.gov/

- Become a Registered user and set up an Electronic Copyright Office (eCO) account at https://www.copyright.gov/registration/

- Complete the online application form, detailing your book and your personal information. https://www.copyright.gov/gruw/

- Pay the registration fee. https://www.copyright.gov/about/fees.html

- Submit a copy of your book, either digitally or as a hard copy. https://www.copyright.gov/registration/

- Copyright registration FAQ https://www.copyright.gov/eco/faq.html

3. Deciding on Pricing and Royalty Options

Pricing:

Consider the following when setting your book's price:

- Cost of production.

- Comparable titles in your genre or field.

- The perceived value of your book.

- Distribution and retailer discounts.

Royalty Options:
Royalties are payments made to authors for the sale or use of their books. Different publishers or platforms offer varying royalty rates. Consider:

- The distribution channel (e.g., Amazon Kindle Direct Publishing, IngramSpark).

- Print costs, if applicable.

- The country of sale.

4. **Other Pre-Publishing Considerations**

- **Barcodes:** Often, print books need a barcode representing the ISBN and sometimes the price.

- **Legal Deposits:** Some countries require you to deposit copies of your book with a national library or similar institution.

- **Age Ratings:** For children's or YA books, ensure the content is suitable for the target age range.

5. **Libel and the Importance of Fact-Checking**

Libel:
Libel involves making false statements in written form that harm someone's reputation. Avoid making false or damaging statements about identifiable individuals or entities.

Fact-Checking:
Always fact-check your work. This not only adds to the credibility of your book but also helps you avoid potential legal pitfalls. Consider:

- Hiring a professional fact-checker.

- Citing your sources clearly.

- Using primary sources wherever possible.

Conclusion:

In conclusion, understanding and navigating the legalities and formalities of publishing are as crucial as the creative writing process itself. Ensure that all aspects are handled meticulously to prevent future complications. Always consult professionals when in doubt, especially regarding legal matters.

Notes:

_____

_____

_____

_____

_____

_____

_____

_____

_____

_____

_____

_____

Notes:

_____

_____

_____

_____

_____

_____

_____

_____

_____

_____

_____

_____

_____

_____

_____

_____

_____

_____

_____

_____

_____

Notes:

_____

_____

_____

_____

_____

_____

_____

_____

_____

_____

_____

_____

_____

_____

_____

_____

_____

_____

CHAPTER
EIGHT

CHOOSING a PUBLISHING ROUTE

In the age of the Internet, getting a book published has never been more accessible. There are now multiple avenues authors can pursue to bring their work into the world. However, choosing the best publishing route can feel overwhelming with so many options at hand. This chapter seeks to simplify the process by laying out the fundamental differences between traditional publishing and self-publishing, guiding you through the world of agents and book proposals, and offering insights into various self-publishing platforms.

1. **Traditional Publishing vs. Self-Publishing**

   - **Traditional Publishing**

     - **Pros**:

       - Financial backing: Publishing houses cover costs associated with editing, design, distribution, and some marketing.

       - Professional team: Experienced editors, cover designers, and marketing teams to guide and help refine your work.

       - Credibility and reputation: Being associated with an established publisher can offer an implied seal of approval.

- Distribution: Easier access to major bookstores and international markets.
- **Cons**:
  - Time: The traditional publishing process can be lengthy—from finding an agent, to securing a deal, to the book release.
  - Loss of rights: Authors typically sign away some or all rights to their work, potentially limiting future adaptations or changes.
  - Royalties: A smaller percentage of sales go to the author, often between 10-15% for physical books.
- **Self-Publishing**
  - **Pros**:
    - Control: Full creative and business control over content, design, pricing, and more.
    - Speed: Once your book is ready, it can be on the market in a matter of days or weeks.
    - Royalties: Authors keep a more significant portion of sales, often upwards of 60% on certain platforms.
  - **Cons**:
    - Initial costs: Authors shoulder upfront costs for editing, cover design, formatting, and potential marketing.

- Distribution: More challenging to get into brick-and-mortar stores.

- Stigma: Some still perceive self-published works as less prestigious, although this is changing.

2. **Agents and Book Proposals**

If you opt for traditional publishing, the first step is often finding a literary agent. Agents are professionals who represent authors, pitching their client's books to publishers, negotiating contracts, and ensuring the best deals.

- **Finding an Agent**:

    - Research: Look for agents who specialize in your book's genre or topic.

    - Query letters: A letter pitching your book to potential agents. Be concise, professional, and engaging.

    - Patience: Finding an agent can take time. Rejections are standard, but perseverance is key.

- **Book Proposals**:

    - Needed for non-fiction: While fiction books are usually sold based on a complete manuscript, non-fiction is often sold on a proposal.

    - Components: Overview, target audience, comparative titles, chapter outline, sample chapters, and marketing strategy.

3. **Platforms for Self-Publishing: A Comparison**

There are multiple platforms available to self-publish your work, each with its strengths and limitations.

- **Amazon Kindle Direct Publishing (KDP)**:

    - Pros: Huge audience, seamless integration with Amazon, favorable royalty rates for certain price points.

    - Cons: Some exclusivity clauses, especially if you opt into Kindle Unlimited.

- **Apple iBooks**:

    - Pros: Access to Apple's ecosystem, no exclusivity.

    - Cons: Requires an Apple device for direct publishing, fewer marketing tools.

- **Smashwords**:

    - **Pros:** Wide distribution to multiple retailers, no exclusivity.

    - **Cons:** Lower visibility compared to Amazon or Apple.

- **Barnes & Noble Press**:

    - **Pros:** Direct access to the B&N audience, physical printing options.

    - **Cons:** Smaller market share compared to Amazon.

- **Others (Kobo Writing Life, IngramSpark, etc.)**: Each platform will have its benefits and challenges. Consider factors like royalty rates, distribution options, and ease of use.

Conclusion:

In conclusion, whether you choose traditional publishing or self-publishing, remember that each route has its unique benefits and challenges. Consider what you value most, be it creative control, potential earnings, or the prestige and support of a traditional publisher. Your publishing journey is unique, and the best route is the one that aligns with your personal and professional goals.

Notes:

_____

_____

_____

_____

_____

_____

_____

_____

_____

_____

Notes:

Notes:

_____

_____

_____

_____

_____

_____

_____

_____

_____

_____

_____

_____

_____

_____

_____

_____

_____

_____

_____

Notes:

_____

_____

_____

_____

_____

_____

_____

_____

_____

_____

_____

_____

_____

_____

_____

_____

_____

_____

_____

_____

CHAPTER
NINE

LAUNCHING and MARKETING

Your book is a labor of love, but if no one knows about it, all that hard work could go unnoticed. Launching and marketing your book effectively can make the difference between a bestseller and a book that collects dust on shelves. In this chapter, we'll delve into strategies to propel your book to success from the moment it hits the market.

1. **Building a Launch Team:** A launch team consists of dedicated and passionate individuals who will champion your book. They provide initial reviews, generate buzz, and help spread the word.

   - **Identifying Potential Team Members:** Begin with your inner circle—friends, family, and acquaintances. Also, consider your early readers, beta readers, or anyone enthusiastic about your project.

   - **Engaging Your Team:** Regularly communicate with them, provide them early access to your book, and make them feel involved so they can to leave reviews, share on social media, and spread the word.

2. **Setting Up Pre-Orders:** Pre-orders can drive early sales and create excitement.

   - **Platforms:** Utilize HOV Publishing, Amazon, Barnes & Noble, and other online retailers for setting up pre-orders. Amazon allows for pre-order setups that can boost your book's ranking on day one.

- **Incentives:** Offer bonuses or exclusive content to those who pre-order to boost numbers.

3. **Creating a Buzz:** Leverage various platforms to generate excitement.

- **Social Media:** Tease content, share chapter except, engage with readers, and book cover reveals.

- **Press Releases:** If you have contacts in media, draft a press release detailing the upcoming launch. Send releases to local newspapers, magazines, and online publications related to your book's topic.

4. **Hosting a Launch Event or Virtual Tour:** In the digital age, both physical and virtual book launches can generate substantial interest.

- **Physical Launch:** Organize a physical event at bookstores, libraries, churches or community centers and invite influential figures, and engage local media.

- **Virtual Launch:** Organize a live event on platforms like Zoom or Facebook Live, featuring readings, Q&As, and guest appearances. Coordinate with bloggers, podcasters, and influencers to feature your book during a set period.

5. **Strategies for Getting Reviews:** Reviews are essential for visibility and credibility.

- **ARC (Advance Reader Copy) Distribution:** Send out ARCs to potential reviewers well before launch.

- **Engage Review Platforms:** Platforms like Goodreads and NetGalley can be invaluable.

6. **Leveraging Podcasts, Blogs, and Other Media Outlets:** Guest appearances on media outlets can increase your reach.

   - **Identify Suitable Channels:** Choose those relevant to your book's genre or theme. Offer to write guest posts or provide valuable content in exchange for a book feature.

   - **Prepare a Pitch:** Tailor each pitch to the medium's audience.

   - **Attend and Participate:** In conferences, webinars, and other industry events.

7. **Building Anticipation: Pre-Launch Strategies:** This phase is all about stirring interest and desire.

   - **Cover Reveals:** A well-timed reveal can spike interest.

   - **Share Teasers:** Or excerpts from your book.

   - **Email Campaigns:** Engage your mailing list with updates and behind-the-scenes content. Offer sneak peeks or early access to those who sign up for your mailing list or newsletter.

   - **Host Q&A sessions:** AMAs (Ask Me Anything), or webinars about the topics in your book.

8. **Harnessing Social Media for Promotion:** Social media platforms offer unprecedented access to vast audiences.

   - **Paid Ads:** Platforms like Facebook and Instagram allow targeted advertising.

- **Engage with Followers:** Create shareable graphics or quotes from your book. Regular updates, polls, and interactive sessions keep your audience engaged. Engage in relevant groups or forums to discuss themes from your book.

- **Collaborate**: With influencers to host giveaways or features.

9. **Book Blog Tours and Author Interviews** Leverage the reach of established blogs and platforms.

   - **Identify Relevant Blogs:** Consider genre, audience size, and engagement.

   - **Coordinate**: with multiple bloggers to feature your book over a set period, creating a "tour" of your book online.

   - **Seek Out:** Interviews on podcasts, YouTube channels, and other media platforms. Offer exclusive content or interviews.

   - **Provide**: Unique content or insights for each platform to keep your audience engaged.

10. **Launch Day: Executing a Successful Launch**
    The culmination of your efforts.

    - **Engage All Channels:** Ensure that your social media, email list, and other platforms are buzzing with activity.

    - **Run Promotions:** Or discounts for a limited time to spur initial sales.

    - **Celebrate:** While it's a day of hard work, don't forget to take a moment to celebrate your achievement.

Conclusion:

In conclusion, the launch and marketing phase of your book's journey is as crucial as the writing process. With the right strategies in place, you can ensure your book gets the attention it deserves. Remember, it's not just about the initial launch, but maintaining momentum post-launch. Keep engaging with your readers, seeking opportunities to promote your book, and always be ready to adapt to new marketing trends and tools.

Notes:

_____

_____

_____

_____

_____

_____

_____

_____

_____

_____

_____

_____

Notes:

Notes:

_____

_____

_____

_____

_____

_____

_____

_____

_____

_____

_____

_____

_____

_____

_____

_____

_____

_____

_____

Notes:

_____

_____

_____

_____

_____

_____

_____

_____

_____

_____

_____

_____

_____

_____

_____

_____

_____

_____

_____

_____

CHAPTER
TEN

POST-LAUNCH and BEYOND

The world of publishing doesn't end when your book is out on the shelves, digital or physical. It's an ongoing process, a journey that continues long after the initial excitement of the launch. Here, we'll delve into what comes next.

1. Gathering and Responding to Reviews

Once your book is out in the world, reviews will start to trickle in. These can be both a source of joy and apprehension. Remember, every piece of feedback can be a tool for growth.

- **Gathering Reviews:** Actively solicit reviews. Reach out to readers through social media, email, and other platforms. Many readers don't review unless prompted. Additionally, consider sending copies to bloggers and reviewers in your genre. Understand that not all reviews will be positive. Each reader brings their own perspective and biases.

- **Handling Negative Feedback:** Not all reviews will be positive. When you encounter criticism, consider if there's a constructive takeaway. If readers point out factual inaccuracies or issues, acknowledge them. However, avoid getting into heated debates. It's often counterproductive. Use these reviews as tools for growth. Constructive criticism can be a gold mine for areas of improvement.

- **Thanking Reviewers:** A simple "thank you" can go a long way. It shows appreciation and fosters a positive relationship with your audience.

2. **Keeping the Momentum Going: Post-launch Marketing**

The initial launch period is vital, but maintaining interest is crucial for long-term success.

- **Host Events:** Book readings, seminars, or webinars can keep interest alive.

- **Engage on Social Media:** Use your social media platforms, mailing list, and website blog to update readers about any events, book signings, or related news. Share snippets, behind-the-scenes content, or related articles to keep your audience engaged.

- **Discounts and Promotions:** Periodic discounts can revive interest in your book.

3. **Exploring Additional Revenue Streams: Audiobooks, Translations, Courses**

- **Audiobooks:** With the rise of platforms like Audible, an audiobook version can significantly boost your earnings.

- **Translations:** If your book gains popularity, consider getting it translated to reach a wider audience.

- **Courses:** If your book is informational, turning it into an online course can be a lucrative option.

4. **Considerations for a Series or Subsequent Books**

- **Listen to Your Readers:** They might love certain characters or want to know more about a specific storyline.

- **Consistency is Key:** Ensure the tone, style, and quality are consistent across books.

- **Planning Ahead:** If you're considering a series, sketch out the overarching plot in advance.

5. **Leveraging Your Book for Other Opportunities**

- **Speaking Engagements:** Use your book as a stepping stone for public speaking opportunities, workshops, or as a subject matter expert.

- **Consultation Services:** If your book is on a niche subject, offer consulting services related to that topic.

- **Merchandising:** Depending on your genre, branded merchandise can be a revenue stream and a marketing tool.

6. **Reflections and Preparing for Your Next Book**

- **Assess the Journey:** Take stock of what worked and what didn't.

- **Stay Updated:** The publishing world is evolving. Keep abreast of the latest trends and tools.

- **Begin Again:** Armed with the knowledge from your previous experience, start your journey for the next book. Every book is a new adventure, and every adventure brings its own set of learnings.

Conclusion:

Launching a book is just the beginning. The post-launch phase can be as challenging as the initial steps, but with careful planning and a commitment to continuous engagement, you can ensure your book continues to be in the spotlight long after its release.

Notes:

_____

_____

_____

_____

_____

_____

_____

_____

_____

_____

_____

_____

_____

_____

_____

_____

_____

_____

_____

Notes:

_____

_____

_____

_____

_____

_____

_____

_____

_____

_____

_____

_____

_____

_____

_____

_____

_____

_____

_____

_____

Notes:

_____

_____

_____

_____

_____

_____

_____

_____

_____

_____

_____

_____

_____

_____

_____

_____

_____

_____

_____

_____

CHAPTER
ELEVEN

CONCEPT 2 INCOME™

"A concept is the birth of an idea, but income is its validation in the real world."

Turning Your Literary Brainchild into a Revenue Stream

After pouring hours of labor and vast amounts of creativity into your book, it's natural to hope that it will generate some income. Whether you're aiming for a bestseller or simply want to cover the costs of publishing, understanding how to turn your book concept into income is crucial.

In this chapter, we will explore the journey from completing your manuscript to monetizing it.

1. From Pages to Profits: A Brief Overview

Before diving deep, it's essential to understand the lifecycle of a book's income generation. The journey comprises:

- Initial sales from a launch

- Ongoing sales through strategic marketing

- Residual income through updates, series, or spin-offs

- Ancillary income through related products, events, or services

2. Setting Realistic Expectations

Many authors dream of overnight success. While it's not impossible, it's rare. Understanding the book market, analyzing your target audience, and setting achievable goals is crucial for sustained success.

3. Launch Strategy

Your book's launch can make or break its future sales trajectory. Consider these steps:

- **Pre-launch buzz:** Engage potential readers through teasers, book trailers, and social media campaigns.

- **Launch promotions:** Limited-time offers, discounts, or bonuses can boost initial sales.

- **Engage influencers:** Seek endorsements or reviews from influential people in your genre or industry.

- **Press Releases:** Share your story with media outlets relevant to your book's subject.

4. Online Platforms

Being on popular platforms increases visibility. Ensure your book is available on:

- Amazon Kindle
- Apple iBooks
- Barnes & Noble Nook
- Kobo, and others.

Remember, each platform has its promotional programs like Kindle Unlimited or KDP Select. Understand the pros and cons before enrolling.

5. Diversify with Audiobooks and Podcasts

The audiobook industry is booming. Consider turning your book into an audiobook using platforms like ACX. Podcasts can be used for interviews, book excerpts, or related discussions.

6. Ancillary Products and Spin-offs

If your book offers valuable knowledge or a captivating world, consider:

- Online courses or workshops
- Merchandise (like T-shirts, mugs, etc.)
- A book series, novellas, or short stories

7. Personal Branding

As an author, you're not just selling a book; you're selling yourself. Engage with readers through:

- Author websites and blogs
- Guest postings or articles
- Social media presence and interaction

8. Public Appearances and Events

Events such as book signings, lectures, or workshops can boost sales. While it might sound traditional, the personal touch can often lead to loyal readership.

9. Licensing and Foreign Rights

Licensing your book for adaptations (like movies or series) or selling foreign rights can be a significant source of income. It might be a long shot for many, but for some, it's a game-changer.

10. Regularly Update and Market

The book world is ever-evolving. Regularly updating content, cover design, or pricing can lead to renewed interest. Also, constant marketing, whether through ads, collaborations, or reader engagements, is crucial.

Conclusion

Turning your concept into income requires a blend of creativity, strategic thinking, and perseverance. It's not just about writing; it's about understanding the market, engaging with your audience, and constantly evolving. Remember, the journey of a book doesn't end in publication. It's just the beginning.

Notes:

_____

_____

_____

_____

_____

_____

_____

_____

_____

_____

Notes:

Notes:

Notes:

_____

_____

_____

_____

_____

_____

_____

_____

_____

_____

_____

_____

_____

_____

_____

_____

_____

_____

_____

Notes:

_____

_____

_____

_____

_____

_____

_____

_____

_____

_____

_____

_____

_____

_____

_____

_____

_____

_____

_____

_____

CHAPTER
TWELVE

INTRODUCING AI to the 90-DAY BOOK CREATION

"The rise of AI doesn't necessarily mean the end of the pen, it's just another tool to harness for your creativity."

Introduction:

The last decade has witnessed a significant transformation in the realm of technology, and Artificial Intelligence (AI) is at the forefront of that change. Writers, just like professionals in various other fields, have begun to understand and utilize the potential of AI to streamline, enhance, and expedite the book writing process. In this chapter, we will explore how to integrate AI into your 90-day book creation journey.

1. AI for Research and Information Gathering:

Gone are the days when writers had to spend hours, or even days, at libraries or trawl through the internet for pertinent information. Today's AI tools can:

- Scour the internet for specific data.
- Summarize lengthy articles or journals.
- Validate facts instantly.

Tools to Consider: DeepSearch, Quillbot, and OpenAI's platforms.

2. Writing Aids and Grammar Checkers:

Instead of waiting for an editor to highlight passive voice, punctuation errors, or complex sentences, AI-powered grammar checkers can offer instant feedback.

Tools to Consider: Grammarly, ProWritingAid, and Hemingway Editor.

3. Plot Development and World Building:

AI tools can provide:

- Suggestions for plot twists.
- Descriptions for fictional worlds.
- Character backstories based on brief inputs.

Tools to Consider: Plotly, StoryStream, and Archivos.

4. Productivity Boosters:

Stay focused and keep track of your writing progress with AI:

- Set word count targets.
- Analyze the sentiment and tone of your writing.
- Understand the readability score.

Tools to Consider: FocusWriter, Write With Transformer, and Otter.ai.

5. AI as Co-Writer:

Some writers are now partnering with AI to co-write books. Input a theme or concept, and the AI can generate several pages of content which can then be curated, edited, and refined by the human author.

Tools to Consider: OpenAI's GPT series, Jasper, and Writesonic.

6. Design and Layout:

Use AI tools for:

- Book cover design suggestions.
- Layout and formatting.
- Visualization of scenes or characters for added content.

Tools to Consider: Canva's Magic Resize, BookWright, and RelayThat.

7. Audience Targeting and Marketing:

Once the book is ready, AI can:

- Analyze market trends.
- Predict audience preferences.
- Optimize marketing campaigns.

Tools to Consider: K-lytics, BookBub Ads, and Google's AI tools.

The Ethical Implications:

While AI offers many advantages, it's crucial to understand the ethical side. Always credit AI tools when used, especially if large portions of content are generated. Maintain originality, and don't let AI replace the human touch that makes stories resonate with readers.

Conclusion:

Integrating AI into your 90-day book creation can streamline many aspects of the writing process. From initial research to final marketing, AI can be a formidable ally. However, always remember, while AI can assist, the heart, soul, and voice of your book will always be uniquely human. Happy writing!

Notes:

_____

_____

_____

_____

_____

_____

_____

_____

_____

_____

_____

_____

_____

_____

_____

Notes:

_____

_____

_____

_____

_____

_____

_____

_____

_____

_____

_____

_____

_____

_____

_____

_____

_____

_____

_____

_____

Notes:

_____

_____

_____

_____

_____

_____

_____

_____

_____

_____

_____

_____

_____

_____

_____

_____

_____

_____

CONCLUSION

The culmination of our 90-day journey is not an end, but rather a beginning. These past days have been an expedition of revelation, introspection, and evolution. When we first embarked on this path, the destination might have seemed daunting and remote. Yet, with each passing day, as the pages filled and the chapters formed, the dream of becoming an author inched closer to reality.

Reflecting on these three months, it's evident that this has been more than just about writing a book. It's been about discovering one's voice, confronting fears, and embracing vulnerabilities. Writing, in its very essence, is an act of opening oneself to the world, of sharing stories, dreams, and even the odd nightmare. It's a testament to the human spirit's resilience and its insatiable desire to express, connect, and inspire.

Being an author isn't a title, but a journey—one that extends far beyond the confines of these 90 days. While the process we've undergone has given birth to a book, it has also birthed a new identity for you: that of a storyteller. The journey of an author is lifelong. Every life experience, every observation, and every moment of reflection adds a new layer to the narratives you will craft in the days, months, and years to come.

I encourage you not to see this conclusion as an endpoint but as a stepping stone. Embrace the curiosity that drove you to start this journey, and let it guide you towards continued growth and exploration. Let the world be your muse, and may every interaction, every journey, and every dream be a potential story waiting to be penned.

In the act of becoming an author, you have not only empowered yourself but also have taken on the potential to empower others. Through your words, readers can be transported, transformed, and even transcended. Such is the magic of the written word.

To all the aspiring writers reading this, always remember: the mightiest of forests springs from a single seed. Your first book, your first chapter, or even your first sentence is that seed. Nurture it, believe in it, and let it grow. In doing so, you're not just authoring a book; you're authoring your destiny.

Keep writing, keep dreaming, and above all, keep believing in the power of your story.

APPENDIX

1. Checklists and Timelines

There are several software applications and tools that are specifically designed for or are commonly used for creating checklists and timelines. Here's a list of some of them:

Checklist Creation Tools:

1. **Trello:** A popular visual collaboration tool that offers a card-based system for managing tasks, projects, and checklists.

2. **Todoist:** A task management application that allows users to create tasks, sub-tasks, and checklists.

3. **Microsoft To Do:** A task management tool by Microsoft, it lets users create checklists and tasks.

4. **Wunderlist (before its acquisition by Microsoft):** Was a popular checklist application, though it's been succeeded by Microsoft To Do.

5. **Google Keep:** A note-taking service developed by Google which includes checklist functionality.

6. **Evernote:** A note-taking application that also offers checklist functionality.

7. **Notion:** An all-in-one workspace tool which provides functionality for notes, databases, and checklists among other features.

8. **Checklist.com:** A web-based tool specifically for creating, sharing, and organizing checklists.

9. **Process Street:** An advanced checklist tool that supports more complex processes and workflow automation.

Timeline Creation Tools:

1. **Microsoft Project:** Offers robust project management tools, including Gantt chart creation for timelines.

2. **Toggl Plan (formerly Teamweek):** A visual planning tool that offers timeline and Gantt chart functionalities.

3. **Asana:** A task and project management tool which has timeline views for visualizing project progress.

4. **Timeline Maker Pro:** Software dedicated to making professional timelines with customization options.

5. **Lucidchart:** A visual collaboration tool that offers timeline templates among its various diagramming options.

6. **Smartsheet:** Combines spreadsheet functionality with project management tools and offers Gantt charts for timeline views.

7. **Preceden:** A web-based tool for creating timelines for projects.

8. **Office Timeline:** An add-in for Microsoft PowerPoint, it allows users to create, manage, and display timelines right within PowerPoint presentations.

9. **Time.Graphics:** A free online service for creation of timelines and infographics.

10. **GanttPRO:** Online Gantt chart software for project management which offers a way to visualize timelines.

How to create a project timeline:

Step 1:   Understand the scope of your project.

Step 2:   Split the project into milestones.

Step 3:   Estimate the time of each task.

Step 4:   Assign tasks to your team.

Step 5:   Choose your project timeline software.

Step 6:   Plot each task on your timeline.

Conclusion:

Depending on the specific requirements, features, and functionalities you need, you might opt for one tool over another. Some of the above tools are more suited for personal use, while others are designed for more complex professional or organizational contexts.

2. **Sample outlines and writing schedules**

Here is a sample outline along with a potential writing schedule:

Sample Outline: Novel

A. Introduction
   - Protagonist introduction
   - Setting description
   - Introducing the primary conflict

B. Rising Action
   - Protagonist's first obstacle
   - Introduction of supporting characters
   - Development of secondary plotlines

C. Climax
- Protagonist confronts main antagonist or primary challenge
- Peak of emotional tension

D. Falling Action
- Consequences of the climax
- Resolution of secondary plotlines

E. Conclusion
- Protagonist's final state or transformation
- Resolution of primary conflict
- Final thoughts and setting description

Sample Writing Schedule: Novel

Week 1-2:	Research and planning
Week 3-4:	Write Introduction
Week 5-8:	Write Rising Action
Week 9:	Write Climax
Week 10:	Write Falling Action
Week 11:	Write Conclusion
Week 12-14:	First round of editing
Week 15-16:	Beta reader feedback
Week 17-18:	Final edits and proofreading

3. **Sample 90-day writing and publishing calendar.**

Here's a sample 90-day writing and publishing calendar to keep you on track:

Day 1-30: Pre-writing and Planning Phase
Day 1-5: Research and Brainstorming
- Identify your target audience.
- Research popular topics and trends in your niche.
- Brainstorm potential article/book topics.

Day 6-10: Outline and Structure
- Create a rough outline for your piece(s).
- Determine your writing process (do you need quiet? Certain tools? Specific times of day?).

Day 11-15: Gather Resources
- Identify key resources, references, or research you'll need to write.
- Create a mood board or inspiration list if helpful.

Day 16-30: First Draft
- Begin writing your draft. Aim for a certain word count per day to stay on track (e.g., 500-1000 words/day for a longer piece, or one article every two days for shorter pieces).

Day 31-60: Writing and Initial Revisions Phase
Day 31-45: Continue Drafting
- Finish your first draft if it's not done yet.
- Allow for days when you might not meet your word count but make up for it the following day.

Day 46-50: Break from Writing
- Take a few days off to rest and distance yourself from your work. This will allow you to approach it with fresh eyes during the revision phase.

Day 51-60: **First Round of Revisions**
- Start with larger issues like structure and content flow.
- Fix any obvious errors or inconsistencies.
- Consider having a peer review or a beta reader give feedback.

Day 61-90: Final Revisions, Editing, and Publishing Phase
Day 61-70: **Final Revisions**
- Refine based on feedback and your own rereading.
- Focus on fine-tuning your language and ensuring clarity.

Day 71-75: **Professional Editing (if possible)**
- If you can, have a professional editor review your work.
- Implement their feedback.

Day 76-80: **Final Read-through and Formatting**
- Make sure your work is formatted appropriately for its publishing platform (e.g., ebook formatting, blog post visuals, etc.).
- Conduct a final read-through.

Day 81-85: **Prepare for Publishing**
- If it's an article, prepare any associated media (images, videos, etc.).
- If it's a book, consider your publishing options (self-publishing platforms, traditional publishers, etc.).
- Prepare a marketing or promotion plan.

Day 86-90: **Publish and Promote**
- Publish your work on your chosen platform.

- Share on social media, email newsletters, or other promotional avenues.
- Engage with your audience, responding to comments or feedback.

Conclusion:

Remember, this is just a sample calendar. Depending on the nature and complexity of your writing project, the timeframes might need adjustment. Always consider your personal pace, available resources, and the specific needs of your project.

4. Templates: Email pitches, press releases, etc.

Below are a few different templates for email pitches, press releases, and more. You can use these as starting points and modify them to fit your specific needs.

Email Pitch to a Blogger/Influencer

Subject: Exciting Collaboration Opportunity with [Your Brand/Company Name]

Hi [Blogger/Influencer's Name],

I hope this email finds you well. My name is [Your Name] and I work for [Your Brand/Company Name]. We've been following your [blog/Instagram/YouTube channel] for some time now and are consistently impressed by the quality of your content and the engagement you receive.

We feel that a collaboration between [Your Brand/Company Name] and your platform would be mutually beneficial. [Briefly describe your product/service]. We'd love to offer you [specific collaboration details: e.g., "a free product for review," "a sponsored post opportunity," etc.]

Please let us know if this interests you, and we can discuss further details.

Warm regards,

[Your Name] [Your Job Title] [Your Company's Website]

Press Release Announcement

FOR IMMEDIATE RELEASE

[Your Company Name] Contact:
[Your Name] Email:
[Your Email] Phone:
[Your Phone Number]

[Your Company Name] Announces [Major News or Product Launch]

[CITY, STATE, Date] – [Your Company Name], a leading [industry and specialty], is excited to announce [major news or product launch]. This new [product/service/development] showcases [key features or benefits].

[2-3 paragraphs detailing the news or product launch, its significance, quotes from company representatives, and any other relevant information.]

About [Your Company Name] [1-2 paragraphs about your company, its history, mission, and significant achievements.]

For more information about [the announcement or your company], please contact [Your Name] at [Email] or [Phone Number].

Networking Email

Subject: Exploring Opportunities - Let's Connect!

Hi [Name],

I hope this note finds you well. My name is [Your Name], and I work in [Your Profession/Industry]. I came across your profile on [LinkedIn/Industry Event/Recommendation] and was truly impressed by your background in [specific aspect of their work].

I'm currently exploring opportunities in [specific area/field] and would value a chance to discuss your experience and insights over a virtual coffee or call.

Would you be available sometime [next week/over the next couple of weeks] for a brief chat? I promise to keep it short and respect your time.

Thank you for considering my request, and I look forward to the possibility of connecting.

Best regards,

[Your Name] [Your Contact Information]

Conclusion:

These templates are just starting points. It's essential to personalize and tailor them to fit the unique context and needs of each situation.

5. **Different Types of Advertising**

Advertising can take on various forms, depending on the medium, audience, and objectives. Here are some of the primary forms of advertising:

1. **Print Advertising**: This includes advertisements in newspapers, magazines, brochures, and flyers. It's one of the traditional forms and can target local to international audiences depending on the publication.

2. **Broadcast Advertising**: This encompasses TV and radio ads. TV ads can offer a blend of sight, sound, and motion to make a compelling case, while radio ads rely on sound.

3. **Outdoor Advertising**: Billboards, banners, and transit advertisements (e.g., on buses, trains) fall under this category.

4. **Digital/Online Advertising**:

   - **Display Ads**: Visual ads shown on websites.

   - **Search Engine Advertising**: Ads that appear in search results (e.g., Google Ads).

   - **Social Media Advertising**: Ads on platforms like Facebook, Instagram, Twitter, etc.

- **Email Marketing**: Sending promotional content directly to people's inboxes.

- **Content Marketing**: Creating valuable content to attract and retain an audience, often subtly promoting a brand.

- **Affiliate Marketing**: Promoting products for other companies and earning a commission on sales.

- **Video Advertising**: Ads that play before, during, or after online videos.

5. **Direct Mail Advertising**: Sending physical promotional material directly to people's homes or businesses.

6. **Telemarketing**: Over-the-phone advertising where products or services are pitched.

7. **Point-of-sale Advertising**: Promotions or ads that are placed near the checkout counter in a store.

8. **Product Placement**: Integrating products into movies, TV shows, or other media content so that they appear as part of the scene.

9. **Influencer Advertising**: Collaborating with influencers (individuals with significant online followings) to promote products or services.

10. **Guerrilla Advertising**: Unconventional advertising strategies that aim to achieve maximum results with minimal resources. Often surprising and unconventional, they rely heavily on creativity.

11. **Native Advertising**: Ads designed to match the look and feel of the media format they appear in. They don't appear as traditional advertisements and often come across as content.

12. **Sponsorships**: Brands can sponsor events, athletes, or programs, ensuring visibility during the event or broadcast.

Each form has its own advantages and challenges, and the choice often depends on the target audience, objectives, and budget.

6. **Advertising Resources and Tools**

However, if you're looking for a general list of tools and resources that are commonly associated with different types of advertising, here's a basic overview:

1. **Digital Advertising:**

   - **Ad Platforms:** Google Ads, Facebook Ads Manager, Instagram Advertising, Twitter Ads, LinkedIn Ads.

   - **Analytics Tools:** Google Analytics, Facebook Pixel, Mixpanel, Hotjar.

   - **Design Tools:** Canva, Adobe Creative Cloud (Illustrator, Photoshop), Sketch.

   - **Landing Page Builders:** Unbounce, Leadpages, Instapage.

   - **Ad Testing:** Optimizely, VWO.

2. **Print Advertising:**

- **Design Tools:** Adobe InDesign, QuarkXPress.

- **Print Brokers:** PrintingForLess, MOO, Vistaprint.

- **Distribution Services:** USPS Every Door Direct Mail.

3. **Broadcast (TV and Radio) Advertising:**

- **Production Tools:** Adobe Premiere Pro, Final Cut Pro.

- **Audience Measurement:** Nielsen Ratings, Comscore.

4. **Outdoor (Billboard) Advertising:**

- **Design Tools:** Adobe Illustrator, Photoshop.

- **Providers:** Clear Channel Outdoor, Lamar Advertising, Outfront Media.

5. **Search Engine Marketing (SEM):**

- **Keyword Research:** Google Keyword Planner, SEMrush, Ahrefs.

- **Management Tools:** Google Ads Editor, Bing Ads Editor.

6. **Search Engine Optimization (SEO):**

- **Analysis Tools:** Google Search Console, MOZ, SEMrush, Ahrefs.

- **On-site SEO:** Screaming Frog, Yoast SEO (for WordPress).

7. **Email Advertising:**

   - **Email Platforms:** Mailchimp, SendinBlue, Constant Contact, ConvertKit.

   - **Design Tools:** BeeFree, Stripo.

   - **A/B Testing:** Litmus, Email on Acid.

8. **Affiliate Marketing:**

   - **Platforms:** ShareASale, ClickBank, CJ Affiliate.

   - **Tracking Tools:** Post Affiliate Pro, Voluum.

9. **Influencer Marketing:**

   - **Platform & Tools:** AspireIQ, Upfluence, BrandSnob, Traackr.

10. **Content Marketing:**

    - **Content Management Systems:** WordPress, HubSpot, Joomla, Drupal.

    - **Content Creation:** Grammarly, Hemingway Editor.

    - **Content Distribution:** Outbrain, Taboola.

11. **Podcast Advertising:**

    - **Hosting Platforms:** Libsyn, Anchor, Podbean.

    - **Ad Networks:** Midroll, Podgrid.

12. **Retargeting/Remarketing:**

- **Platforms:** Google Ads (Remarketing), Criteo, AdRoll.

Conclusion:

This is just a basic overview, and there are many other tools and platforms available for each type of advertising. The best choice often depends on the specific needs and objectives of a campaign.

ABOUT THE AUTHOR

 Germaine Miller-Summers is a dream revitalizer. She has the innate ability to listen to one's passions and goals, and generously pour her inspiration, resources, and innovation into their vision. More importantly, a believer that faith without works is dead, she brings accountability and an unbiased lens to every creative idea that is introduced to her. Her objectivity allows her to provide crucial constructive criticism and foresee potential barriers to success. She is an energized and empathetic multi-media strategist who has mastered the skill set of helping others obtain access to the hard-to-reach dreams and capabilities in their life. She is an experience, and she is waiting for you!

A leader who wears not too many but just enough hats, she is also the founder and CEO of HOV, LLC with the rapidly growing divisions of Hope of Vision Publishing and HOV Media, LLC a Multi-Media Consulting Firm. For more than 16 years, Hope of Vision Publishing has worked with hundreds of authors to publish and promote more than 500 books. From novice writers to best-selling authors, her clients rely on Hope of Vision Publishing to provide a seamless publishing experience built on her long-held values of integrity, quality, and customer service. It is why authors return to Hope of Vision Publishing year after year.

Hope of Vision Publishing offers its clients an array of publishing services. Whether it's editorial coaching for first-time authors, ghostwriting and editing, audio and video transcription, or post-publication marketing and public relations support – the company provides a complete and customized publishing experience.

Equipped with a degree from the world-renowned Fashion Institute of Technology (FIT) in New York City. Her experience and marketing savvy led her to manage artists like The Lox and the late DMX. With more than 25 years of honing her skills in the entertainment industry and a desire to create something of her own; Mrs. Miller-Summers was called and excited to help others create their own creative excellence.

Miller-Summers endeavors are comprehensive, but of all her services, the most valuable is her ability to "midwife," evoke, market, and maintain her clients' visions and then turn them into a reality. "Through her businesses and celebrating one's vision, Germaine Miller-Summers helps to give voice to the obscure."

CONNECT WITH US

HOV Publishing:
Website: https://hovpub.com
Email: hopeofvision@gmail.com

HOV Media, LLC:
Email: hopeofvisionmedia@gmail.com

Hope of Vision Connect Podcast:
Subscribe to the YouTube Channel:
https://www.youtube.com/@HopeofVisionConnect?sub_confir
mation=1
Website: https://hovpub.com/hov-connect-podcast
Email: hovconnectpodcast@gmail.com

Social Media:
Instagram: @hovconnect
Facebook Group.com: @hovconnect
Facebook: @GermaineMiller-Summers
Linked-In: @Germaine Miller-Summers
TikTok: @ExperienceGermaine

HOV Publishing Academy:
Email: hovpacademy@gmail.com
Email: 90daybookcreation@gmail.com

HOV Markets:
Website: https://hovmarkets.com/
Email: hovaffiliate@gmail.com

Experience Germaine: Consulting/Coaching
Email: experiencegermaine@gmail.com